## An Italian Meal

The different dishes in an Italian meal are usually served as separate courses.
The first course may be pasta, risotto or soup, followed by a second course of fish or meat.
A vegetable dish often comes with or after the second course, followed by a simple green salad.
Cheese and fruit then end the meal.
What variety!

Salute!

# Italian Favorites

Antipasti 1
  Caponata (eggplant) 2
  Roasted Red Peppers 3
  Zucchini Sticks 4
  Crostini or Bruschetta (garlic bread) 5-6

First Courses
  Spaghetti with Garlic Sauce 7
  Linguini with Clams 8
  Fusilli with Red Pepper Sauce 9
  Penne with Sausage 10
  Tuna with Marinara Sauce 11-12
  Orecchiette (or Sea Shells) with Broccoli 13
  Fettuccini with Shrimp and Scallops 14
  Lasagne 15
  Baked Ziti 16
  Ravioli 17
  Maccheroni Vegetable Stew 18
  Minestrone 19
  Risotto 20-21
  Polenta 22-23

## Second Courses
Chicken Cacciatora — 24
Breaded Chicken with Tomatoes & Basil — 25
Chicken Breasts with Lemon & Parsley — 26
Roast Chicken with Potatoes & Rosemary — 27
Swordfish (or Tuna) with Mint — 28
Braciolone (stuffed and rolled steak) — 29-30

## Other Dishes
Baked Eggplant Mozzarella (side dish) — 31
Baked Beans Tuscan-style (side dish) — 32
Zucchini Frittata (breakfast or light supper) — 33
Tuna & Bean Salad (lunch or light supper) — 34
Ricotta Pudding (dessert) — 35


Italian Cheeses; which to use when — 36

S. J. Fretz

♻ printed on recycled paper          *calligraphy by p. dutery*

# Antipasti ("before the meal")

Italian appetizers, called antipasti (the plural of antipasto) are seen more often in restaurants than in Italian homes, where an antipasto is usually very simple, such as thin slices of prosciutto, and slices of melon or ripe figs.

Italian American restaurants more often serve an antipasto that combines many colorful, artistically arranged appetizers, such as:

- anchovy fillets
- marinated artichoke hearts
- marinated mushrooms
- black or green olives
- salami, sliced wafer thin
- prosciutto, sliced wafer thin
- sliced cheese, such as provolone
- quartered hard-cooked eggs
- pickled hot peppers
- sliced tomatoes
- radici (radishes)
- celery hearts
- lettuce
- caponata (eggplant), roasted peppers and zucchini sticks (pages 2, 3, 4)

## Caponata (eggplant)

Serves 8 as part of an antipasto platter, 4 as an appetizer.

1 pound eggplant, peeled and cut into ½" cubes
5 tablespoons olive oil
2 stalks celery, coarsely chopped
1 medium-large onion, finely chopped
¼ cup balsamic vinegar
1 tablespoon sugar
1 cup skinned ripe tomatoes,* or canned Italian plum tomatoes, chopped
8-10 capers, rinsed and cut in half
6 large green Italian or Greek olives, chopped
2 tablespoons pine nuts

Sprinkle eggplant with salt and drain in colander ½ hour. Rinse, drain and dry on paper towel. Heat 2 tablespoons oil in a non-stick skillet. Sauté celery and onion for 10 minutes. Remove and set aside. Add enough oil to skillet to make 3 tablespoons. Sauté eggplant for 10 minutes. Stir in vinegar and sugar. Return celery and onions and add tomatoes, capers and olives. Reduce heat. Cover and cook 5 minutes. Turn into bowl, stir in pine nuts and chill.

* To skin tomatoes, place in boiling water for ½ minute. Skins will peel off easily.

## Roasted Peppers

Roasted, peeled sweet peppers are delicious and eye-pleasing in antipasto and salads. Red ones are sweeter, more attractive and easier to peel than green, but mixing them together, perhaps including a yellow one, makes a smashing presentation.

To roast, hold the peppers with tongs over the flame of a gas burner, turning often, or line up under a broiler flame and turn often with tongs until charred or blistered on all sides. When cool enough to handle, peel off the skin with your fingers. Remove and discard core and seeds and cut flesh into strips.

For an antipasto, mix the pepper strips with chopped olives, chopped anchovies, capers, pine nuts and minced garlic. Marinate overnight in a small amount of extra virgin olive oil. Top with chopped parsley before serving.

Roasted pepper strips are also good as a topping for crostini or bruschetta (page 5) or as a salad, dressed with olive oil and lemon juice. If desired, mix with skinned (page 2) tomatoes, chopped.

# Zucchini Sticks

*Serves 4 as part of an antipasto platter, 2 as an appetizer.*

½ pound zucchini
vegetable oil for deep frying
6 tablespoons flour
salt, pepper and garlic powder to taste

Peel and scrub zucchini and cut into "French fries" 3 or 4 inches long and ¼" to 3/8" across. Pour oil ¾" deep in a skillet or large pot and heat to 375° over high heat. For batter, pour ½ cup water into a small bowl. Sift flour through a sieve into the water, stirring constantly until smooth. When oil is hot, dip zucchini into batter, then drop into oil, using only enough zucchini to make one layer without crowding. Cook until golden, then remove to paper towel. Repeat until all zucchini is fried. Be sure oil temperature does not drop. Sprinkle with salt, pepper and garlic powder.

# Crostini or Bruschetta

Crostini is the original Italian garlic bread: sliced, oven toasted and brushed with olive oil. Grilled, it is called bruschetta (pronounced bruce-ketta). Instead of serving this bread with a meal, Italians serve it as part of an antipasto, or an appetizer or snack.

Because it is so simple, this dish must be made with the best ingredients: traditionally baked Italian bread (or at least, good French bread), extra virgin olive oil and fresh garlic. The bread need not be fresh. This is a good way to use day-old Italian bread just past its prime.

For basic crostini or bruschetta, cut the bread into ½" thick slices and toast in a 400° oven for 10 or 12 minutes until golden, or on a grill until golden. Rub one side well with a fresh peeled garlic clove (you will see the garlic oil come off on the hot bread) and brush or drizzle with olive oil. That's all!

Italians also dress-up these "little toasts" with an endless variety of toppings, such as: (page 6)

## Toppings for Crostini or Bruschetta

- A light coating of anchovy paste, or chopped, mashed anchovies
- Roasted red pepper strips (page 3)
- Thinly sliced fresh tomatoes topped with chopped, fresh basil
- Chopped sun-dried tomatoes
- Freshly grated Parmesan or Romano cheese (page 36)
- Goat cheese
- Shredded mozzarella, melted under a broiler
- Cannellini beans (Italian white beans), mashed and mixed with minced garlic, olive oil, sage and salt and pepper.
- Olive paste:
  Pit ½ cup black Italian or Greek olives. Combine with 2 anchovy fillets, 1 or 2 large garlic cloves, crushed, and 2 teaspoons rinsed capers. Mince and mix in a bowl with 2 tablespoons olive oil. Spread sparingly on toasts.

## Italian Pasta

All these recipes call for dried pasta, preferably imported from Italy, as American pasta tends to turn mushy when cooked. A pound of dry pasta with sauce serves 4 or 5 as a main course, 6 to 8 as a first course.

## Spaghetti with Garlic Sauce

1 pound spaghetti
½ cup olive oil
4 large cloves garlic, minced
*2 eggs, beaten
*½ cup freshly grated Parmesan cheese
freshly ground black pepper to taste
½ cup chopped Italian parsley

Cook spaghetti according to package directions. While spaghetti cooks, heat oil in a small frying pan and cook garlic over very low heat until it turns a light golden color. Remove from heat and pour over drained spaghetti. Quickly stir in eggs and then the cheese. Transfer to a serving bowl, add pepper and parsley, and toss.
*This is just as good made without the eggs and cheese.

# Linquini with Clams

4 dozen littleneck or small cherrystone clams
1/3 cup olive oil
4 large cloves garlic, minced
3/4 cup chopped Italian parsley
1/2 teaspoon freshly ground pepper

1 pound linquini
1 loaf Italian bread (optional)

Scrub clams and set aside.
Heat oil in large pot. Add garlic, parsley and pepper and simmer 2 minutes. Add clams, bring to a boil, reduce heat, cover and simmer until shells open (5-10 minutes). Stir occasionally. While clams cook, prepare linquini according to package directions. To serve, divide linquini into individual bowls. Top each portion with clams, and pour sauce over all.

Serve with a loaf of hot, crusty Italian bread for diners to dip chunks of the bread into the sauce lingering in the bottom of their bowls.

---

Curly parsley, sold in most markets, may be substituted for the flat-leafed Italian parsley. Although similar in taste, the Italian parsley has more "bite."

# Fusilli with Red Pepper Sauce

¼ cup olive oil
4 medium-large onions, chopped (about 4 cups)
3 large red bell peppers, chopped
1 pound fusilli (spiral-shaped pasta)
1 cup chicken or vegetable broth
¾ teaspoon dried red pepper flakes (optional)
salt and freshly ground black pepper to taste
½ cup freshly grated Parmesan or Romano cheese

Heat oil in a large heavy skillet. Add onions and peppers and sauté about 20 minutes, until well cooked but not brown. While sauce cooks, cook fusilli according to package directions. Add broth and red pepper flakes to cooked onions and peppers and cook 5 minutes. Purée in food processor. Return to skillet and reheat. If desired, thin with a little broth or water. Toss with fusilli and serve. Pass the cheese at the table.

Tip: Reduce broth by half a cup for a thicker sauce, and serve over broiled or baked fish.

# Penne with Sausage and Broccoli

2-2½ pounds broccoli rabe (page 13)
3 tablespoons olive oil
2 cloves garlic, minced
1 pound sweet Italian sausage, made without fennel or spices
¾ pound short, tubular pasta, such as penne
salt and freshly ground black pepper
1 lemon, quartered

Cut off and discard bottom half of broccoli stems. Cut remaining broccoli into 2" lengths. Steam (in 2 batches) 5 minutes, until soft but not limp. Remove to large bowl. Heat 1 tablespoon oil in a large, non-stick skillet. Add garlic and cook until golden. Add to broccoli. Place sausage in skillet and brown. Break into 2" lengths and add 1 tablespoon water. Cover and sizzle gently for 15 minutes, until cooked.
Cook pasta according to package directions. Before serving, combine broccoli and garlic with sausage and heat 2 minutes. Using a slotted spoon, return mixture to bowl.
Add pasta, 2 tablespoons oil, salt and pepper to skillet. Stir well to combine with juices in skillet. Divide among 4 plates and top each with sausage and broccoli, and a wedge of lemon on the side.

# Tuna with Marinara Sauce

1 pound linguini

2 tablespoons olive oil
2 large scallions (white part and 2" or 3" of green), thinly sliced
2 large cloves garlic, minced
2 cups marinara sauce (page 12)
2 tablespoons lemon juice
1 pound fresh tuna, cut into bite-size chunks

1 bunch arugula leaves (about 6-8 ounces) cut in half crosswise, or ½ cup chopped Italian parsley
pinch hot red pepper flakes
⅓ cup (about 20) pitted and chopped black gaeta or Greek olives

Cook linguini according to package directions. Drain and pour into a large bowl. Meanwhile, heat oil in a large skillet and sauté scallions and garlic 2 or 3 minutes, until soft. Add sauce and lemon juice and bring to a boil. Reduce heat, add tuna and simmer 5 minutes or until fish is opaque. Add remaining ingredients, stirring to cover leaves with sauce, and cook 1-2 minutes or until arugula is softened but not wilted. Pour over linguini, toss and serve.

## Marinara Sauce

This basic tomato sauce is good on pasta, eggplant, chicken, fish or Italian sausage. It keeps well and may be frozen. Commercial sauce may do in a pinch, but homemade is always better.

Makes about 4 cups

1 cup olive oil
2 large cloves garlic, minced
3 medium onions, finely chopped (about 2 cups)
1 large carrot, finely chopped
2 stalks celery, finely chopped

1 35-ounce can Italian plum tomatoes
¼ teaspoon pepper
1 tablespoon chopped basil, or 1 teaspoon dried
2 tablespoons butter (optional)
⅛ teaspoon sugar
½ teaspoon salt (if tomatoes are salt-free)

Heat oil in large skillet. Add next 4 ingredients and cook 10 minutes over medium heat. Push tomatoes and juice through a sieve (to remove seeds) and stir into vegetables in skillet. Add remaining ingredients and simmer 30 minutes.

Variations: For a velvety smooth sauce, purée cooked sauce in a food processor.

For a darker sauce, cook vegetables until brown before adding tomatoes.

# Orecchiette with Broccoli Rabe

Broccoli rabe (pronounced "rob" or "rop"), has a pungent taste, more leaves, and less flower than standard American broccoli. You may use regular broccoli for this dish but it won't have as much zing. Orecchiette ("little ears") is a disc-shaped pasta about the size of a thumbnail. Pasta shells of a similar size may be substituted.

1½ pounds broccoli rabe
1 pound orecchiette or pasta shells
½ cup olive oil
3 or 4 large garlic cloves, minced
3 anchovy fillets or 2" anchovy paste
¼ teaspoon dried red pepper flakes
½ cup freshly grated Romano cheese

Cut off and discard bottom ⅓ to ½ of broccoli stems. Wash remaining broccoli and cut into 1" to 1½" lengths. Steam or boil 3 minutes and set aside. Cook pasta according to package directions. While pasta is cooking, heat oil in a large skillet. Add garlic and cook until light golden. Add anchovies, mash and mix with oil. Add broccoli and pepper flakes. Cook 5 minutes, stirring. Drain pasta, mix with broccoli and stir in cheese. Intense!

# Fettuccini with Shrimp & Scallops

4 tablespoons olive oil (or 2 tablespoons oil and 2 tablespoons butter)
3 cloves garlic, minced
½ cup dry white wine
½ cup bottled clam juice

1 pound fettuccini

1 cup canned Italian tomatoes, without juice
pinch hot red pepper flakes
1 tablespoon fresh thyme or 1 teaspoon dried
¼ cup chopped Italian parsley
salt and freshly ground black pepper
¾ pound shrimp, peeled and deveined
¾ pound scallops (if large, cut in half)

Cook garlic in hot oil in large skillet until light golden. Add wine and clam juice and boil rapidly for 5 minutes, to reduce. Add tomatoes, hot pepper, thyme, parsley, salt and pepper. (Break tomatoes apart with wooden spoon.) Cook another 5 minutes, or longer, until thickened. Cook fettuccini according to package directions. When pasta is almost done, add shrimp and scallops to skillet. Cook, stirring once or twice, until shrimp and scallops turn opaque (about 2 minutes). Drain pasta, turn onto serving platter and top with contents of skillet.

# Tri-color Lasagna
## In the colors of the Italian flag!

White sauce: 6 tablespoons sweet butter
6 tablespoons flour
3 cups milk
salt and pepper to taste
¼ teaspoon nutmeg

red pepper sauce (page 9), using ½ cup broth and no pepper flakes
1 pound undercooked spinach lasagna noodles
1 cup freshly grated Parmesan cheese

Preheat oven to 375°. Melt butter in saucepan over low heat. Add flour, stir well and remove from heat. In another pan, heat milk to just below a boil. Return butter and flour to low heat. Add milk, all at once. Stir 10 minutes. Stir in salt, pepper and nutmeg. Oil a 9"x 13" glass baking dish. Coat lightly with white sauce. Add a layer of overlapping noodles, then half the red pepper sauce, another layer of noodles, half the remaining white sauce and ½ cup cheese. Add a third layer of noodles, the remaining red sauce, then the remaining white sauce. Top with remaining Parmesan. Place in oven, reduce heat to 350° and cook ½ hour.

# Baked Ziti

Serves 4-6

1 pound ziti

6 tablespoons butter
1 cup heavy cream
8 tablespoons freshly grated Parmesan cheese
1 pound mozzarella cheese, shredded
8 tablespoons chopped Italian parsley
2 cups marinara sauce (page 12), warm
freshly ground black pepper to taste

Preheat oven to 400°. Cook ziti. Drain, return to pot and cover.
Melt butter in large heavy saucepan over medium heat. Stir in cream and 6 tablespoons of the Parmesan cheese. Add about ¼ of the mozzarella cheese and stir until cheese melts. Add ziti, stirring well to coat. Stir in 6 tablespoons parsley, 1¾ cups marinara sauce and pepper. Transfer mixture to a shallow baking dish and top with remaining mozzarella. Bake 10 minutes, or until mozzarella is melted, but not brown. Top with remaining sauce, Parmesan and parsley.

# Ravioli

*Serves 2*

An old legend has it that Marco Polo introduced Italy to pasta after encountering noodles on his famous voyage to China. Now we know that Italians were making pasta long before Marco Polo's time! But in this age of global interchange, we borrow Chinese wontons to make delicious thin-skinned ravioli. It's easier than making your own pasta dough!

1 cup ricotta cheese
¼ cup freshly grated Parmesan cheese
1 cup fresh basil leaves, chopped
salt and pepper to taste
24 wonton squares
1 egg, beaten

Bring a large pot of water to a boil. Mix together cheeses, basil, salt and pepper for filling. Working quickly, lay out 12 wonton squares and drop a tablespoon of filling in the middle of each. Brush each remaining square with egg and lay egg-side-down on top of a filled square. Press edges together to seal. If desired, brush top with egg and fold corners to make a diamond shape. Drop into boiling water for 3 minutes. Remove with slotted spoon to paper towel. Top with sauce (page 12) or melted butter and Parmesan.

# Maccheroni Vegetable Stew

*Serves 4*

4 tablespoons olive oil
1 large onion, chopped
1 green bell pepper, chopped
2 cloves garlic, minced
2 stalks celery with leaves, chopped
1 small hot chili pepper, finely chopped
1 large or 2 small carrots, chopped
1 small-to-medium zucchini, chopped

2 cups cooked or canned chick peas
1 16-ounce can Italian tomatoes
½ cup chopped Italian parsley
½ teaspoon each dried oregano, rosemary, basil
8 ounces elbow macaroni, uncooked

½ cup freshly grated Parmesan cheese

Heat oil in large heavy pot or skillet. Cook vegetables over moderate heat until soft, 10-15 minutes. Add liquid from chick peas and tomatoes with enough water to make 3 cups. Add chick peas, tomatoes, parsley and seasonings. Bring to a boil. Stir in macaroni. Cover and boil gently for 10 minutes. Stir, cover and set aside for 20 minutes, stirring again after 10 minutes. Serve with Parmesan cheese and freshly ground black pepper.

# Minestrone

*Serves 6-8*

¼ cup olive oil
2 large cloves garlic, minced
1 large onion, chopped
2 medium carrots, chopped
3 stalks celery, chopped
2 medium potatoes, peeled, cut into ¼" cubes
1 cup green beans, sliced
3-4 cups shredded cabbage
1 16-20 ounce can Italian plum tomatoes
salt and pepper to taste
½ teaspoon each dried basil, rosemary and sage
2 cups cooked white beans (or canned)
¾ cup elbows or other small macaroni
½ cup freshly grated Parmesan cheese

In a large pot, heat oil to medium-high. Add garlic and onion. Sauté 2 minutes. Add carrots and celery. Cook 3 minutes. Add potatoes and green beans. Cook 3 or 4 minutes. Add cabbage, tomatoes, salt, pepper, herbs and 8 cups water. Bring to a boil, cover, reduce heat and simmer 3 hours. Add beans, bring to a boil, add macaroni and boil gently 15 minutes. Stir in cheese.

---

Buy Parmesan cheese in wedges and grate just before using. Save the "heel" that's left and add to soup when adding water.

It's no wonder that Americans have taken to Italian pasta; it's so versatile and easy to cook. But other basic starch dishes, such as risotto and polenta, are beloved by Italians also, and just as versatile. They do require constant stirring at the last minute, so try them first as one-dish meals or accompanied with dishes that can be prepared ahead of time.

## Risotto

Risotto must be made with short grain Italian rice, such as arborio, sold at any Italian grocery.

5 cups home-made chicken broth (or ½ canned broth mixed with ½ water)

¼ cup olive oil
1 small onion, finely chopped
1½ cups arborio rice
½ cup freshly grated Parmesan cheese
1 tablespoon butter (optional)

Keep broth at a low simmer on a back burner. Heat oil in a large heavy saucepan. Add onion and cook until soft. Add rice and cook, stirring, 2-3 minutes. Add ½ cup broth and cook, stirring, until rice absorbs the broth. Continue to add broth ½ cup at a time, as previous amount is absorbed, stirring constantly to avoid sticking. The entire process should take 25-30 minutes with the pot at a constant simmer. You may not need all the broth. When done, the grains of rice should be creamy outside and slightly chewy inside. Stir in cheese and optional butter before serving.

<u>Variations:</u>
For a complete one-dish meal, stir in a cup of cooked shrimp or scallops and a 12-ounce package of thawed frozen peas for the last few minutes of cooking.

Rinse 1 ounce imported dried wild mushrooms and soak them 30 minutes in 1 cup warm water. After adding 2 cups broth to the rice, add mushrooms with soaking water, ½ cup at a time. (If gritty, strain the water through a coffee filter.) Proceed as in basic recipe, adding broth until done.

Substitute white wine for 1 cup of the broth.

Add 1 teaspoon crumbled saffron threads with the cheese.

Add dried rosemary, sage or thyme with the last ½ cup of broth.

## Polenta

Depending on the occasion and the sauce or topping, this Northern Italian cornmeal staple can serve as a first course, side dish, or one-dish meal. Leftover polenta is delicious for breakfast when sliced and fried in hot olive oil, butter or bacon grease.

Serves 4

5 cups water
2 teaspoons salt
1½ cups cornmeal

Bring water to a boil in a large, heavy pot. Lower heat and keep water simmering throughout the process. Add salt. Using a wooden spoon, <u>very gradually</u> stir in the cornmeal. One way to control the flow is to pour the cornmeal into a fine sieve held over the pot with one hand. Shake the sieve up and down, while stirring constantly with the other hand. This allows the cornmeal to fall slowly into the water. Keep stirring until all the cornmeal is absorbed, and the mixture begins to adhere to itself rather than the pot. Pour onto a platter, or traditionally, a wooden board. Make a dent in the middle and fill with 4 tablespoons butter and ¼ cup freshly grated Parmesan cheese, or sausage and vegetable sauce (page 23).

# Sausage and Vegetable Sauce for Polenta

3 tablespoons olive oil
1 clove garlic, minced
1 small onion, chopped
1 small carrot, chopped
1 stalk celery, chopped
1 pound sweet Italian sausage, sliced
1 cup canned Italian tomatoes, with juice

Before cooking the polenta, heat oil in a skillet and sauté vegetables until soft. Add sausage and cook 10 minutes, until lightly browned. Add tomatoes, breaking them up with a wooden spoon. Simmer, stirring occasionally, while you make the polenta.

Pour the cooked polenta onto a platter, make a dent in the middle of it and fill with sausage and tomato sauce.

---

Extra virgin olive oil is from the first pressing of the olives, which gives it superior flavor, and therefore is particularly recommended for salad dressings. Heat reduces its flavor, so regular olive oil is just as good for sautéing.

# Chicken Cacciatora

Serves 3-4

1 3-3½ pound chicken, cut into 6-8 pieces
½ cup flour (to coat) mixed with salt and pepper
3 tablespoons olive oil
2 cloves garlic, chopped
1 small onion, thinly sliced (about ½ cup)
½ cup dry wine (white or red)

1 green bell pepper, cut into thin strips
1 medium carrot, peeled and sliced thin, using food processor or hand grater
1 16-20-ounce can Italian tomatoes with juice
½ teaspoon dried sage

Heat oil in large skillet. Turn each chicken piece in flour mixture, shake to remove excess flour and brown in oil on all sides. Remove chicken and set aside. Cook garlic and onion in the same skillet for a few minutes. Add wine and allow to cook down over medium-high heat, about 10 minutes. Stir in remaining ingredients. Return chicken to skillet. Cover, lower heat and simmer until chicken is done, about 30-35 minutes.

# Breaded Chicken Breasts

*Serves 4-6*

3 whole chicken breasts, split, skinned and boned
juice 1 lemon
olive oil
2 medium (under-ripe) tomatoes, sliced

2 eggs, beaten
1 cup dry breadcrumbs
½ pound mozzarella cheese, shredded
2 tablespoons chopped fresh basil or Italian parsley
freshly ground black pepper

Preheat oven to 375°. Slice or pound the chicken breasts to flatten. Marinate in lemon juice for ½ hour. Coat a non-stick baking sheet with olive oil. Add tomato slices, drizzle with more oil and bake ½ hour. Place ¼" olive oil in large skillet and heat. Pat chicken pieces to dry, dip in beaten eggs, then breadcrumbs, and cook in the oil 2 or 3 minutes on each side, until no longer pink inside. As each piece is done, remove to baking sheet and top with a slice of baked tomato and shredded mozzarella. Place under broiler and broil 1 minute to melt the cheese. Sprinkle with herbs and serve with freshly ground black pepper.

# Chicken Breasts with Lemon and Parsley

Serves 4-6

4 tablespoons olive oil
3 whole chicken breasts, split, skinned and boned
juice 1 lemon (about 1/4 cup)
4 tablespoons chopped Italian parsley
salt and freshly ground black pepper

Slice or pound the chicken breasts until uniformly flat. Heat oil in large skillet and sauté chicken breasts over medium heat for 1 minute on each side, or until a knife slit through the thickest spot shows no trace of pink flesh. Remove to a platter and keep warm. Stir lemon juice, parsley and butter into the pan. Heat and pour over chicken, sprinkle with salt and pepper and serve.

Variation: To serve with spaghetti, add 2 more tablespoons of olive oil and lemon juice to pan after removing chicken. Pour sauce over both spaghetti and chicken.

---

Italians make just enough sauce to flavor their pasta, while Americans are apt to serve a little pasta with their sauce.

# Roast Chicken and Potatoes
### Serves 3 or 4

4 cloves garlic
2 tablespoons chopped fresh rosemary, or
   3 teaspoons dried
1 3-3½ pound chicken
4 tablespoons olive oil
3 or 4 medium potatoes, quartered

Preheat oven to 375.° Place 3 cloves garlic and ⅓ of the rosemary in cavity of chicken. Rub outside of chicken with 2 tablespoons olive oil, remaining garlic clove and another ⅓ of the rosemary.
Coat bottom of roasting pan with remaining oil. Place chicken on rack in pan. Arrange potato pieces in pan under sides of rack, turn them in the oil, and sprinkle with the remaining rosemary. Roast for 1 hour, basting the chicken and turning the potatoes every 15 minutes. Add a little more oil if potatoes threaten to stick.

>  Note: If your roasting pan isn't large enough to accommodate the potatoes, they may be cooked in oil in a separate pan.

# Swordfish with Mint

Swordfish and tuna might be called the meat of Southern Italy. The steaks of both fish are often grilled or broiled and flavored with fresh herbs and lemon in a marinade.

Serves 4

1 tablespoon chopped fresh mint
1 tablespoon chopped Italian parsley
2 cloves garlic, minced
3 tablespoons olive oil
juice 1 lemon

2 pounds swordfish (or tuna) steaks

Mix all ingredients, except the fish, in a large shallow glass or ceramic dish. Turn fish in the mixture to coat both sides, and marinate 30-60 minutes, turning once. Remove fish from marinade and grill or broil 5 minutes on each side. Serve with freshly ground pepper and sprigs of mint.

Variation: If using tuna steak, spice up the marinade with ½ teaspoon dried red pepper flakes, 1 tablespoon capers and 10 finely chopped black olives.

# Braciolone

This stuffed rolled meat dish from Southern Italy has many names and many versions. In a land where meat, especially beef, is not abundant, it is usually reserved for special occasions. Traditionally, whole eggs are lined up to form the center of the roll, which makes a stunning presentation when the roll is sliced. However, starting with sliced eggs makes the meat much easier to roll.

Serves 4

## The Sauce

1 onion, finely chopped
2 cloves garlic, minced
¼ cup olive oil
¼ cup tomato paste
1 can (8-ounce) tomato purée
1 large can (28 or 35 ounces) Italian tomatoes
½ cup red wine
salt and pepper to taste

Cook onion and garlic in hot oil until light brown. Add tomato paste and cook, stirring until it darkens. Add remaining ingredients, breaking up tomatoes with a wooden spoon. Simmer 1 hour before adding stuffed meat roll (page 30).

# The Stuffed Meat Roll (continued)

1 slice boneless round or rump steak, about 9"x 12" and 3/8"-1/2" thick. Have butcher trim and pound to about 1/4" thick.
salt and freshly ground pepper
1/2 cup grated Parmesan cheese
1/2 cup chopped Italian parsley
2 cloves garlic, slivered

1 large onion, thinly sliced
1 large tomato, thinly sliced
1 Italian-style green pepper, cut into thin strips
1 stalk celery, cut into thin strips about 3" long
2 hard-cooked eggs, sliced

2 tablespoons olive oil

Sprinkle steak with salt, pepper, cheese, parsley and garlic. Place vegetables and eggs evenly over steak, to within 1/2 inch of edge. Roll up like a jelly roll, tuck in the ends and tie well with kitchen string. Brown on all sides in hot oil. Add to simmering sauce and simmer 1 1/2 hours, turning meat occasionally. Add water, if needed, to prevent scorching. Remove string and slice before serving. Serve with spaghetti.

# Baked Eggplant Mozzarella

This Italian favorite can serve as an antipasto or a side dish. It is equally at home at a feast or with a simple pasta dinner.

1 large eggplant (or enough small ones to total 1½ pounds) peeled or unpeeled
4-6 tablespoons olive oil
¾ cup marinara sauce (page 12)
6 ounces mozzarella cheese, shredded
3 tablespoons freshly grated Parmesan cheese

Slice eggplant and coat both sides of each slice with oil. Broil close to heat about 4 minutes on each side. Turn oven to 325°. Coat a 9"x 13" glass or ceramic baking dish with olive oil and cover with a thin layer of sauce. Place eggplant slices over sauce in 1 layer and top each slice with remaining sauce, then mozzarella, and then Parmesan. Bake 15 minutes or until very soft.

# Fagioli al Forno
Tuscan-style baked beans.

1 pound dried white beans, preferably Italian cannellini beans (about 2 rounded cups)
2 large garlic cloves, chopped
¼ pound piece pancetta or prosciutto (Italian ham), chopped
½ teaspoon crumbled dried sage leaves
3 tablespoons olive oil
2 ripe (or canned) Italian plum tomatoes, chopped
salt and pepper to taste

Rinse beans well, removing any foreign matter. Soak overnight or for several hours in 6 cups cold water. When ready to cook, drain and discard water. Preheat oven to 375°. Mix beans and all other ingredients in a casserole with enough water to cover. Cover and bake until done, about 2-2½ hours. After 1 hour of cooking, stir every half hour.

# Zucchini Frittata

This slow-cooking Italian omelet will serve 4 as a light supper or a Sunday breakfast. Sliced mushrooms may be added, or substituted for the zucchini.

6 eggs
salt and pepper to taste
2 tablespoons chopped fresh basil or Italian parsley
4 tablespoons freshly grated Parmesan cheese

4 tablespoons olive oil
1 medium-large onion, thinly sliced
2 small zucchini, thinly sliced
2 tablespoons butter or oil

Beat eggs until smooth. Add salt, pepper, herbs and 3 tablespoons cheese. Set aside. Heat oil in a large skillet. Add onion and cook 2 minutes. Add zucchini and cook 2 minutes more to brown. Reduce heat and cook another 5 minutes. Remove with slotted spoon, dry with paper towel and stir into egg mixture. Melt butter in the same skillet. Pour in egg mixture and cook over very low heat for 15-20 minutes, until set but slightly runny on top. Sprinkle with remaining cheese and broil 1 minute to set top. Cut into wedges and serve.

# Tuna and Bean Salad

*Serves 4*

Southern Italians eat a lot of tuna, both fresh and canned. This popular Italian salad uses canned tuna, but must be made with dried beans, as canned ones are too mushy for this treatment.

1 cup (½ pound) dried white beans
1 bay leaf

1 6½-ounce can tuna, packed in oil, drained
1 small red onion, finely chopped

Dressing: ¼ cup extra virgin olive oil
2 tablespoons red wine vinegar
¼ cup chopped Italian parsley
salt and pepper to taste

Place beans in an enamel saucepan with 3 cups cold water. Bring to a boil. Cook 2 minutes. Cover and remove from heat for one hour. Add bay leaf, return to boil, lower heat and simmer 45 minutes to one hour or more, until cooked through but not too soft. Drain. Discard bay leaf and cool in refrigerator for about an hour. Break up tuna and mix with chopped onion, then mix with the beans. Toss with dressing. Serve for a summer lunch or light supper.

## Ricotta Pudding

Most Italian meals end with fruit, but every feast day has its special sweets and pastries. Between the two extremes, this simple treat can please a sweet tooth after a family meal.

*Serves 4*

1 pound ricotta (2 cups)
butter and flour for coating

2 eggs, beaten
½ cup sugar
grated rind, 1 lemon
4 tablespoons rum, or 1 teaspoon vanilla extract
1 teaspoon ground cinnamon
powdered sugar for dusting (optional)

Place ricotta in a colander set over a large bowl. Drain 1 hour and discard drippings.
Preheat oven to 350°. Coat a small baking dish with butter, then dust with flour. Set aside. Combine ricotta, eggs and sugar and beat until smooth. Add lemon rind, rum or vanilla, and cinnamon. Mix well. Pour into baking dish and bake 40 minutes. Dust with cinnamon and powdered sugar before serving.

# Italian Cheeses

The best Parmesan cheese is <u>Parmigiano Reggiano</u>, an aged mellow cheese from the Emilia region of Italy. For maximum fresh flavor, buy in wedges cut from the wheel. Keep in refrigerator, well wrapped (in paper <u>and</u> foil or plastic), and grate as needed.

<u>Romano</u> is a good grating cheese with a sharper flavor than Parmesan. Pecorino Romano, made from sheep's milk, is one of the best.

<u>Ricotta</u> is a moist, unsalted cheese, sometimes called Italian cottage cheese, but much tastier. Used in lasagna and ravioli, it also adds a nice touch to scrambled eggs.

<u>Mozzarella</u>, in Italy, is made from the milk of water buffalo, but Italian-American delis make a good, fresh cow's milk "mutz" that's soft and moist, nothing like the "plastic" mozzarella sold in supermarkets. In the summer, it's delicious with fresh, sliced tomatoes, chopped basil and Italian bread.

<u>Provolone,</u> that deli standby, is fine sliced in sandwiches, or served with antipasto.